Whispers Of The Silent Sea

The Inner Beauty Of The Subconscious Mind

Kamya Konchada

BookLeaf Publishing
India | USA | UK

Made with ❤ on the BookLeaf Publishing Platform
www.bookleafpub.in
www.bookleafpub.com

Dedication

"To the inner emotions of a young mind, the tranquility of nature, and the depths of knowledge and wisdom.

To my family, who have always supported me throughout—your love and belief in me have been my greatest strength.

To my loving friends, who encouraged me and showered me with kindness—your support has been a light in my journey.

This book is the art of the mind, showcasing the insights of deep emotions and the true feelings of the voiceless nature. May these words speak where silence lingers."

Preface

Poetry is the key to open up the aspirations of people of all ages. It helps you revive from the uncertainty of the situations of deep emotions. I believe its the best way to lighten your imagination into a picture. The beauty of poetry is that a reader can interpret it in their own perspective and initiate innumerable thoughts.

In this short journey of my life, I have developed to express my emotions and aspirations in the form of poems. Each poem sets its own purpose of an urge of change to thrive to overcome rage and sorrow. Nature is a priceless gift to mankind, its our duty to protect and appreciate its contributions and sacrifices.

The art of poetry is not about following the law of language or obeying the laws of science. It's about weaving our own laws and enjoying the moment of creating every line of the piece. This book "Whispers Of The Silent Sea" welcomes young writers like you and me, to get inspired and uncover the talents of the young writer within you.

Acknowledgements

A poem would be a piece of account or a story if it's left alone, with no encouragement and appreciation from the readers. Firstly, I would like to express my deepest gratitude to my family who always helped me initiate my talent as a poet and encouraged me to write more. Secondly, to my loving friends who showed their eagerness to read and review my poems and ensured it to be the best piece, by correcting my mistakes and showed the path of improvement. Their appreciation and comments gave me the urge to come up with new ideas for writing poems and use different elements to the poem.

I would also like to thank the writers of "*Write The World*", who inspired me with their writings presenting beautiful meanings and by spending quality time reading and commenting on the poems I have written. They acted as true mentors and reviewers. A special thanks to all the readers of this book, who have been a part of this journey.

With gratitude,
Kamya

1. The Unwavering Thoughts

Its daring dark,
I hear the breath of lifeless air.
The extinguished stars is all I see...
No shifting of the crust.
No dust and no speck of green,
No dripping and no clicking.

The world as we know,
Is in a pause.

You are alone!
The only one,
Said the voice.
Breathing and causing the waves...
In its oscillation.

Did I go into a black hole?
Am I dreaming ?
Why can't I hear the ticking?
Is the Earth out of its axis and stopped rotating?
Is this The End Of The World?

"Come for dinner, its quite late", said my mom

I am back to my own senses
Now I feel the air
The change of atmosphere, gives me a sign of relief.
But HOW LONG WAS I READING THE BOOK?

2. Get Ready To Rise

Prompt: Call for climate action

A tree, as it falls...
We lost the air for the life
How will you live without it?
A factory built, in its place
The impurity, is all you get
There the living falls...
All the green vanished with smoke.

Will you ever rise ?
Will the earth hold it for longer?

The Earth replies...
The ice, losing its form
The shield of three atoms, is in threat.
Humanity, waiting to meet its extinction
The fire rapids up its invasion
And soon I will loose my form.

A wise man in urging for action replies...
The green will flourish 4 times the ashes
The pure liquid, is all you will find
The marathon, will never end
I will teach the invaders a lesson.

The rocky red body is not the aim,
Its the blue of life you got to save,
The depth of the core is the target,
Not the crew off the crust, to the dark.

Sustain The Treasure!
I Am Warning You...
Or else, you will lose it soon...
Open your eyes to see the light.
Time has come for you to begin.
Clear the footsteps of the past.
Create the steps for the present,
The future will meet your prints to save...

Witness The Change
Raise Your Voices
Create The Future
BEFORE ITS TOO LATE...

3. The True Zillionaire

When I was just a little sapling,
I found a seed in a jar of nothing
If I plant the seed, I will be a zillionaire, I thought

I ran and ran...
I found the place
Where no drop
Where no spec of green
Just a kingdom of death and decay

I put the seed beneath the earth
And gave lots of precious liquid

I waited and waited...
I found a green worm from the earth
With no leaf
With no fruit
Just a pinch of green

I gave it lots and lots of the same liquid
And found a leaf on the earth
The joy of the growth
Crept into me

The time ticked
And the leaf turned into leaves
A huge green in front of me

I planted lots and lots of the same around
The dead desert vanished
And the green flourished

I grew and grew...
And felt the richness of the green
Where lots of beings live
Where there is the true treasures of life
I lived in tranquility
I lived a zillionaire...

4. Tranquility

Skies Smokey
Roads Busy
Time Ticking
People Running
Buildings Crashing
Water Flowing Backwards
I am Completely Out Of This Place.

People Do Not Realize My Presence.
I Sit In A Corner,
Waiting For The Movement
To Find A Way,
Through The Brimming Place.

Searching My Way In The Dark,
Making Dwarfish Steps Like A Newborn,
Wondering If I Will Ever Exist,
In The Unpure Soil Of My Evil Twin,
The State Of Turmoil.

The Time Is Ticking...
I Need To Take The Final Leap,
Else, I Will Be No More

A Bright Light Enlightens Me...
I Dominate The Darkness With My Mind.

I Exist In Only One Place,
Where The Skies Are Crystal Clear.
Where I Hear The Dewdrops Slipping From The Leaves,
And The Wind Howling With Joy,
And People Busy In Their Odd Jobs,
Worshiping The Nature.
Living Within Its Boundaries,
Living The Lives Of The Early Beings,
Breathing The Purest Form,
The Nature Has Provided.

I Am The TRANQUILITY
Which Flourishes This Place
With Plentiful Life In Peace!

5. Humans

Prompt: A piece where the stars and planets are people.

Together we pretend (As a solar system)
The reality is alone (The sun is alone and does not depend on anything)
Revolving around the thoughts (The sun is stationary)
I am in fire (The heat and temperature of the sun)

I reflect on other ideas (like the planets use the light of the stars to be visible)
I am nothing without the other
I rise for the half
And rest the half (sun rise and sunset)

6. The Feeling

Prompt: About an unusual texture.

It gives you a shiver
As you keep gazing at it.
The cracks are almost invisible
To your sight
The colors are undefined
With varying gravity
The tasteless emotions,
Hidden with delicacy
Purity is undefined.
As a pigment of nihility
Get the second glance
You will experience a paradise of change.

Like the events of your life flicker,
The emotions of your soul exchange,
The taste of the spices slip,
The appearance is exquisite to express.

The weave of the illustration
Brings the moment in the click.

7. The Change

To my soft dry skin
The thirst satisfied the wither
By the moist cold salt
Sorrow drenched deeply
The flick of the confidence
Swells like the rise of sun
From the depths of the east

8. Scaffolding

Prompt: Seasonal Haiku

As the Lians climb
Steel-strong and weakly lean
The backbone of the soul.

9. Give Life To Science

Science isn't the subject
The science is you
The reality around you
It's not the reactions of the chemistry
It's about the different forms we see
It's not the derivations in physics
It's about the things you see
And the rhythm you hear
It's within you which gives you life
The dopamine you acquire
The illusion of a friend
And the essence of friendship beneath
Deep into the core of the earth
Deep into the sky undefined
Science is the magic
And you are the magician
The musical notes of the past
The code of line of the present
The final product of the future
The science as it disappears

10. The Black Hole

When you imagine the possibilities
The deeper you transverse
The deeper you get lost
Its darker when you lighten
Its savage and starving every nano of a second
Consumes everything around
It will change your course
It controls the universe
Created from the death of a star
Created to clean every spec on its way.
Theories come and go
But the secret is kept within
The hole of danger
The hole with one way
And no path to find
And no particle to breath
Physics of Earth does not exist
This could be the way to another

11. Do You Know?

The world as we know
Know that it's going to end
End with fire or ice?
Ice freezing you to hate
Hate built, demolishes the world
World which suffers fire
Fire invades the world with desire
Desire of the millions
Millions extinguish into the crust
Crust drenched with cracks
Cracks which never heal
Heal the world before it's too late!

12. The Reign Of Tomorrow

As the wind cries lavishly,
As the seismic waves, bang on the shore,
As the crust clutters wide open,
As the ice melts, like a wounded soul,
As the age of fire, begins in fall,
The dry death scales the end.

13. Recovery

The final clasp is what I dreamt
But...
What happened is quite disappointing!
The trust of truth, shuttered into a zillion pieces,
Soul like a fragile glass
As I look into the broken end,
The clutters burnt and never to mend.

The voice of the dead heart, provoked my inner darkness...
This is not the final end!
Find the debris and mend it in,
Begin the future and regret nothing.

Life is weaved in the threads of tangles.
It's about how you unwind it
It's not about how you fall and create more
Let's Begin The New Phase!

14. The Six Senses

The massless clouds of the blue
Damped to the mightiness of the gravity
Is it a play of Atlas? I thought
Flowing the supremacy as a Titan.

The touch of the tear
From the squeeze of the Nimbus
The birth of a feeling,
Flowing from the veins of the soul.

The melody of the clinking
From the jazz of the Clarinet
The swap of the beats,
Flowing from the tips to the roots.

The crystals of the clear
From the tincture of the Quartz
The stare of the flash,
Flowing from the pupil of the natural oculus.

The taste of the earth
From the expertise of the Chef
The delicacy of the rear,
Flowing from the tract of flavor.

The breath of the freshness
From the nature of the Growth
The spirit of the aroma,
Flowing from depths into the quarks.

The tranquility of the time
From the voice of the Larynx
The resonance of the waves,
Flowing from the inflection unheard.

15. The Turning Point

Call of the lonely voice,
For a need of aid and care
For a need of faith and trust
For a need for an answer and a solution.
To an impure soul,
With all the rage and temper
With all the sense of grief and sorrow
With all the thoughts and uncertainty.
To which I answered...
The love of cure and remedy
The love of honesty and sincerity
The love of effort and determination.
In just a change of a hunch,
The change of my mind
The change of a life
The change of my day,
Trapped the impurity.
To drench the deserted state
To gain the power of faith
To enlighten the flourished land
All it takes is a brink of courage.

16. The Relay Race

The throbbing of my heart and mind,
Set me on alert as the barren was passed.
I can feel the adrenaline,
Flowing through my veins.
Every step counts to the win.

The time lapses,
As slow as the snail.
I barely had a particle to breathe.
A sense of shiver in my body,
As a figure passes through,
Reaching the end before me.

Losing no hope to win,
I strengthen my muscles,
To coordinate with my bones.
I increase the fluctuations and the vibrations.

With no visibility and no audibility,
As my inner Darkness,
I only see the finish line.
I raced like a chase of cheetah,
And reached the final end,
With the pride of champion,
The triumph of the team.

17. The State Of Seclusion

The speechless sounds,
The thoughtless dreams,
The touchless feeling,
Dug deep under my own trap.

The legends of this treasure
The inscription wiped,
Under the pour of a tear
Forgotten by all
Before the birth of the cosmos.

Triumph stand the people, I hear
The closer of my chapter, I declare
The lashes of seas interrupts,
The path between the endless seas, as it appears.

As the imprints, I leave behind,
Wasted away leaving no trace
I reach the forgotten land
As impalpable as air.
Floating like a feather or a cloud,
Diminishing beyond the visibility.

Returns the figure
From the waters of blue
To the shore so unique
The memories wiped
I stand as a fresher between the fame.
The mists of the dark
Reminds the win of the change.

18. The Dawn Of A New Chapter

As the sun rises from the east,
The hue of the horizon in yellow and orange,
As the Sunchant calls from its sleep,
The merry colors chant the world.

The silence of the earthy creatures,
Vanished in a dim of light.
As the true spirits evoke,
Like the growth of a sapling.

The vivid dreamers awake,
With soul blissed with the joy of life,
A new day, ignites with new desires
Welcoming the elation of a new birth.

As the tremors start in fall,
As the bloom of spring
Spreads across the living sphere,
Greets the rebirth of a new tale.

19. Death vs Life

Flames ice cold,
Breeze of shooting stars,
Hues of gray and brown,
Diseased the soul to the lost,
Never to be found again.

The seize of motion,
The seize of time,
Locked behind the doors of death,
Terribly ditched beneath.

The crawl of life within the blue,
Extinct like desires extinguished,
Nowhere to be found.
Recorded in the history,
After the dinosaurs,
In the history books...

How did this happen?

Humans brought metals to life,
Made them superior and immortal,
Devastating human loss.

Will this be our next "once upon a time"?

Listen to the chirrupings of the sky.
Breathe the sweetness of the living.
See the reverberation of rapture...

Do you realize something?

Something that can be sustained,
Something that—once lost—
Leaves no trace behind.
Vanished like prints on the shore,
Swallowed by the might of a black hole.

What will our story be then?

The dry death of Mars,
With emptiness in plenty.
No moments, no chaos,
Just tranquil pieces of barren silence.

Or the lavish blue,
With sprinkles of green,
Showering life into every cell,
Hid beneath the fragile sphere,
Blissed with hope and cheer.

20. The Lockdown

Free spirits rise
Beneath the horizon of the vista,
The sense of similar lives,
Under the paths of endless eternity.

Minds of writers, minds of scientists,
Minds of teachers, minds of learners—
The Genius Mind, but contrast in minds.

The change in minds
Is all we require.
The restriction of ability,
For being the same
And never to revise.

A threat of shift alerts them all.
The silence spreads with hollow minds.
Why do they take to the peak?
Why not act sooner and live in peace?

The long-awaited evolution
Obstructed with desires
The sense of carelessness drives the end.
The sense... do you recognize?

The fall of sky,
The rise of ground,
The breath of fire,
The poison of taste,
The occurrence of the future.

A halt will fix the cracks
Like the tree from its soul,
With no seed, with no root,
Just the will to grow.

A true mind
Is neither a writer, neither a scientist,
Is neither a teacher, neither a learner.
It is the mind of simplicity.

The hectic it becomes
As you elongate it for long.
The more easier,
As you thrive it sooner.

Now it's our time
To act as **The Mind**,
Keeping away our fears,
Replacing the labyrinth of a maze,
Applying the desires for a change,
Liberate the dreamers in lockdown.

21. The Highest Civilization

Robots.
Towers automated.
Self-growing society.
Access to all corners:
The ground, the ocean, the sky, and the core.
Even space—no longer tranquil.

Humans in Utopia,
Living like the almighty in the sky,
Connecting to alien friends:
The Solarians, the Martians, the Jovians, the Cryolites...
Controlling the system of solar,
The energy of the celestial creatures,
The source of Dyson's Sphere.

It's just a figment of your imagination.
The reality is quite terribly disturbing:
The ashes of wildfires,
Or the chilled flakes of Alaska.
The war of blood pools,
Or the heaps of desires.
The Earth—into bits of a nibble,
Or the Moon—lost in deep space.

Is this all?
Is this the reality?

The answer is **no**.
The **livaloop to infinity**
Begins no sooner.

The twirls of windmills,
The panels to store light,
The component of drink,
The **ultimate energies**!

Sustainability is a statement.
The truth unfolds tri-elements:
Water, oxygen and nourishment,
Even the ecosystem,
Impossible to replicate.
So why colonies on Mars?
Why space hotels?
Why mining the cosmic bodies?

For the satisfaction of our deepest desires,
Of ownership and belongingness,
Corrupts the nature of mind,
Leaving behind the family.
Leaving behind the homeland.
The mainland of debris.

There is still time to act
Create from the scratch
From the scraps of wreckage
To the “**Highest Civilization**”